This book belongs to

_____

Cupid's ~~Love~~ Fart Arrows

by Humor Heals Us

It was Valentine's Day and Cupid was ready, armed with his arrows. Every thing seemed normal. The sun was shining bright. And people were busy shopping and walking in the park.

Cupid loaded his arrows with his magic love potion.

"Ready? Fire!" Down the first arrow went. It had struck the man right where Cupid was aiming. Cupid began rejoicing until he noticed something odd happening to the guy.

The young man did not fall in love. Instead, he went around releasing farts into the air. Soon enough, everyone scattered.

Hmmm...there must be a mistake, Cupid thought.
So he fired another arrow.
This one struck a young woman as she was walking her dog.
"Yes!" Cupid shouted. "Got her on the first try!"

As Cupid watched her and hoped that all was normal, the young lady began releasing the most putrid gas known to man. People began running for their lives.

"No, no, no. This is not how it's supposed to work," Cupid stomped. One by one, everyone began falling victim to Cupid's farting spells.

Cupid was beside himself. He didn't know what to do. In all of his hundreds of years doing this, an event this disastrous had never happened.

It wasn't until he lifted up the potion bottle that he realized what had happened. It was the WRONG one! He had been dipping his arrows in the FART container.

Cupid dipped his arrows in it and hoped that it would work.

Soon, everyone began falling madly in love with each other.

Made in the USA
Middletown, DE
02 February 2022

60296340R00020